MOTOR MAYHEM

OFF-ROAD RALLIES

KENNY ABDO

Fly!
An Imprint of Abdo Zoom
abdobooks.com

abdobooks.com

Published by Abdo Zoom, a division of ABDO, P.O. Box 398166, Minneapolis, Minnesota 55439.

Printed in the United States of America, North Mankato, Minnesota.
052023
092023

THIS BOOK CONTAINS RECYCLED MATERIALS

Photo Credits: Alamy, Getty Images, Shutterstock
Production Contributors: Kenny Abdo, Jennie Forsberg, Grace Hansen
Design Contributors: Candice Keimig, Neil Klinepier

Library of Congress Control Number: 2022946925

Publisher's Cataloging-in-Publication Data

Names: Abdo, Kenny, author.
Title: Off-road rallies / by Kenny Abdo
Description: Minneapolis, Minnesota : Abdo Zoom, 2024 | Series: Motor mayhem | Includes online resources and index.
Identifiers: ISBN 9781098281472 (lib. bdg.) | ISBN 9781098282172 (ebook) | ISBN 9781098282523 (Read-to-me ebook)
Subjects: LCSH: Automobiles, Racing--Juvenile literature. | Vehicles--Juvenile literature. | Off-road vehicles--Juvenile literature. | Off-road racing--Juvenile literature.
Classification: DDC 796.72--dc23

TABLE OF CONTENTS

OFF-ROAD RALLIES

From the driest deserts to the grimiest mud trails, off-road rallies take fans on the most exciting rides!

Pitting cars, trucks, and motorcycles against each other on the roughest of **terrains** has made off-road rallies popular around the world!

Red Bull
Ford
SafetyCulture
Castrol
YX22 FCE

START YOUR ENGINES

After **World War II**, motorcycle trail racing grew incredibly popular. There were some **checkpoints** along the trail. But riders otherwise took their own routes through the course.

18
ANE 641

The sport evolved to include other vehicles. Many off-road race **circuits** began to pop up from Saudi Arabia to North America!

MAYHEM

Rallies are held in many types of off-road locations and on all kinds of **terrain**, including mud, sand, and snow.

Vehicles such as cars, motorcycles, and **dune buggies** are raced in off-road rallies. Vehicles are **modified** with different tires and engines for each **terrain** type.

Off-road rallies have many different types of races. Two of the most popular are desert and short course racing.

PIAK
HILUX
World No.1 Window Film
ARB
HI-WINGS
ADDITIVES
LIQUI

The Baja 1000 is one of the toughest off-road races in the world. Drivers battle dangerous **terrain**, booby traps, and extreme heat. They must travel 1,000 miles (1,609 km) to reach the finish line!

118

BURNOUT

With many types of **circuits** and different types of off-road vehicles, fans will always rally around the **motorsport**.

can-am
23
MAVERICK
SUSCO
F2
F2 THAILAND RALLY

GLOSSARY

checkpoint – a specific place partway through a race where a driver's time is recorded.

circuit – a racetrack for motorsport races.

dune buggy – a small, lightweight vehicle that has oversized wheels that can travel in sand and over dunes.

modification – making a change to something.

motorsport – a sport involving the racing of motor vehicles, like cars and motorcycles.

terrain – a piece of land having certain features.

World War II – a war fought in Europe, Asia, and Africa from 1939 to 1945.

ONLINE RESOURCES

Booklinks
NONFICTION NETWORK
FREE! ONLINE NONFICTION RESOURCES

To learn more about off-road rallies, please visit **abdobooklinks.com** or scan this QR code. These links are routinely monitored and updated to provide the most current information available.

INDEX